Original title:
The Soft Wings of Sleep

Copyright © 2024 Creative Arts Management OÜ
All rights reserved.

Author: Finn Donovan
ISBN HARDBACK: 978-9916-90-812-9
ISBN PAPERBACK: 978-9916-90-813-6

The Alchemy of Awareness

In the stillness of the mind,
Thoughts like whispers softly unwind.
Each moment a bead on life's string,
Illuminating the truth we bring.

Breathe in the wisdom of the dawn,
Let go of the worries you've drawn.
Embrace the clarity, let it flow,
Awareness deepens, and we grow.

The Embrace of Shadows

In twilight's gentle, deepening hue,
Shadows dance, weaving tales anew.
Secrets linger in the night's sigh,
Whispers of dreams that float and fly.

Embrace the darkness, seek the light,
Every shadow holds a spark bright.
Within the quiet, fears subside,
And in the stillness, hope will bide.

Enchanted by the Unseen

In the rustle of leaves beneath the sky,
Magic lingers where the heart will sigh.
Silent forces sway the unseen,
Crafting wonders where dreams have been.

Listen to echoes that softly call,
Step into realms where spirits enthrall.
In every heartbeat, a world will gleam,
Whispers of love in a timeless dream.

Where Sleep Stories Bloom

In a garden of dreams where shadows play,
Sleep stories weave at the end of the day.
Petals unfurl in the moonlight's grace,
Each tale a comfort, a warm embrace.

With every sigh, a journey unfolds,
Wonders await in the night that holds.
Let go of the day, let the soft night loom,
And wander through realms where sleep stories bloom.

Beneath the Veil of Stars

Night paints the sky with sparkles bright,
Whispers of dreams in soft twilight.
A canvas vast, where secrets dwell,
Beneath the stars, I know them well.

Faint echoes call from worlds afar,
In shimmering light, we find our spar.
Here in the stillness, hearts entwine,
Beneath the veil, our souls align.

Serenity's Gentle Caress

A breeze that dances through the trees,
Brushing our skin like tender leaves.
The sun dips low, a golden hue,
In this calm space, just me and you.

Quiet moments wrapped in light,
Peace enfolds us, holding tight.
Time stands still, as dreams take flight,
Serenity shines, a pure delight.

Silken Shadows of Slumber

Silken threads weave whispered dreams,
In gentle night, the soft moon beams.
Wrapped in warmth, the world drifts away,
In shadows deep, we dare to stay.

Crickets sing their evening song,
As time slips by, where we belong.
In every breath, a lullaby,
Silken shadows, where we lie.

A Dance of Feathered Dreams

In twilight's glow, we take our flight,
With feathered dreams, we chase the light.
A waltz through clouds, so soft and free,
Where imagination meets the sea.

With every beat, the heart takes wing,
A symphony of joy we bring.
In harmony, our spirits soar,
A dance of dreams, forevermore.

Threads of Night's Tapestry

In shadows deep, we find our way,
Where whispers weave in soft ballet.
Stars like gems begin to glow,
Stitching dreams in night's tableau.

Silver moons share secrets bright,
Guiding hearts through velvet night.
Every sigh, a thread so fine,
Binding souls in sacred line.

From twilight's edge to dawn's embrace,
We dance within this starry space.
Each breath a stitch, a tale untold,
In night's embrace, our dreams unfold.

The Calm Before Dawn

Stillness drapes the darkened land,
As shadows rest, hush command.
The world holds breath, time moves slow,
In quiet moments, hope will grow.

A rustle sounds, the breeze takes flight,
Whispers stir beneath the light.
Stars prepare to dim their glow,
Awaiting dawn, the day in tow.

In gentle hues, the sky will wake,
As sunlight spills, the hush will break.
Yet in this calm, our spirits rise,
To greet the day, beneath bright skies.

Harmonies of Hushed Moments

In silence sweet, we find our peace,
Each beat of time grants us release.
The stillness sings a soothing song,
Where hearts aligned, we both belong.

Gentle laughter paints the air,
Memory's touch is everywhere.
Softly shared, the whispered dreams,
In hush of night, the spirit gleams.

Underneath the starry dome,
We weave the threads of love's true home.
In each embrace, a world unfolds,
As quiet stories gently told.

Catching Wishes on Starlit Breezes

With hands outstretched, we seek the night,
To catch our wishes in fading light.
The breeze carries tales of yore,
Whispered secrets, longing for more.

Each star a hope, a distant gleam,
Drifting softly on moonlit beam.
In this dance of dreams so bright,
We find our path, guided by light.

Embracing shadows, we dare to dream,
As wishes twirl in quiet stream.
On starlit whispers, our hearts align,
In the vastness, love's pure design.

Nocturnal Embrace

In shadows deep, where silence grows,
The stars awake, their gentle glow.
A whisper calls, the night unfolds,
In velvet arms, a story told.

The moon drapes light on slumbering trees,
A dance of dreams rides on the breeze.
Beneath the veil of starlit skies,
Hearts entwine, where stillness lies.

The Quietude of Midnight

When clocks strike twelve, the world stands still,
The air is thick with a soothing chill.
Soft shadows creep, the darkness sways,
In quietude, the spirit plays.

Time hesitates in this serene hour,
Each heartbeat blooms, a flower's power.
Where thoughts drift free like scattered leaves,
The night enfolds, the soul believes.

Cocooned in Tranquility

Wrapped in softness, a silken embrace,
The world outside fades, a distant place.
Gentle whispers float through the air,
In cocooned peace, we shed our care.

Shimmering stars weave dreams so bright,
As we drift deeper into the night.
In this haven, all worries cease,
Together we find our lasting peace.

Murmurs of the Moonlight

The moonlight dances on rippling streams,
A symphony of soft, tender dreams.
Murmurs echo through the forest deep,
Carrying secrets the night shall keep.

Branches sway to a lullaby's tune,
While fireflies twinkle 'neath the pale moon.
In nature's arms, we lose our fears,
Embracing whispers that calm our tears.

Muffled Secrets of the Night

In shadows deep, the whispers creep,
Silent truths that darkness keeps.
Stars above in quiet glow,
Guarding tales that none may know.

The moonlight casts a silver veil,
Softening all that starts to pale.
Hidden dreams that softly sigh,
Unraveled tales as hours fly.

The cool breeze carries silent pleas,
Rustling leaves in ancient trees.
Gentle voices, sweetly blend,
Muffled secrets, ever tend.

To hearts that listen, calm and wide,
Where mysteries in silence hide.
Embrace the night, the stories call,
In the shadows, we find them all.

Whispers of the Night

The stars stretch wide across the sky,
Whispers dance as breezes sigh.
In the hush, the world slows down,
Lost in dreams, we gently drown.

Night enfolds with tender grace,
Veils of darkness, soft embrace.
Secrets shared in shadows glow,
Where the timid whispers flow.

Moonlit paths of silent grace,
Guiding hearts to find their place.
Each soft murmur, sweet and low,
Carrying tales from long ago.

Embrace the night, let worries cease,
In the hush, we find our peace.
With every star, a wish ignites,
A symphony of whispered nights.

Lullabies in Twilight

As day retreats, the night draws near,
Softly singing, calm and clear.
Twilight hushes, bids farewell,
In its arms, we softly dwell.

Crickets chirp a gentle tune,
Underneath the watching moon.
Colors fade to shades of gray,
As the night takes light away.

Hearts now gather, dreams to share,
In the stillness, secrets bare.
Lullabies in whispers laced,
Wrap us gently, warm and chaste.

Close your eyes and drift away,
Let the night its magic play.
In the twilight, lost in dreams,
Life unfolds in silent beams.

Dreamcatcher's Embrace

Woven threads of starlit night,
Casting dreams in peaceful flight.
Through the webs, the shadows speak,
In their hold, the lost can seek.

Softly swaying, thoughts unwind,
As the darkness gently finds.
Capturing dreams both wild and free,
Held with care, eternally.

In the silence, spirits flow,
Carrying whispers, soft and low.
Every tear, a story spun,
Entwined in hope till night is done.

Rest your head where dreams take flight,
Beneath the cover of the night.
In this embrace, let worries cease,
Find your solace, find your peace.

The Gentle This and That of Night

The moon whispers softly in the dark,
Stars blink like candles, a spark.
Shadows dance lightly on the ground,
In these gentle hours, peace is found.

Cool breezes carry the scent of dreams,
Nighttime holds all its silent themes.
The world sleeps beneath a starry cloak,
In softest hushes, the night has spoke.

Crickets sing sweetly, a lullaby tune,
Silver beams cast by the shy moon.
Time drifts slowly like a drifting leaf,
Within the stillness, we find belief.

Rest now, dear heart, let worries take flight,
Embrace the gentle, this and that of night.
Let slumber wrap you, tender and light,
Till dawn unveils a new day bright.

Drift in a Sea of Night

Sailing through whispers of velvet dusk,
The horizon swallowed in twilight's musk.
Waves of shadows, gentle and wide,
In this deep sea, I choose to glide.

Stars like lanterns are scattered above,
Guiding my journey, a lullaby of love.
Breezes brush softly, a lover's caress,
In the sea of night, I find my rest.

Reflections shimmer on the surface rare,
Tales of wonders drift through the air.
Time feels suspended, a moment of grace,
In this endless ocean, I find my place.

So let me drift, let me wander free,
In the embrace of night's gentle sea.
With dreams as my sails, I'll navigate on,
Till the night whispers and fades with dawn.

A Nest of Restful Moods

Cocooned in warmth, I close my eyes,
Wrapped in peaceful, soft goodbyes.
A nest of thoughts, calm and serene,
Where every whisper feels like a dream.

Feathers of silence gather around,
In this stillness, solace is found.
The world outside blurs into a haze,
Lost in these gently swirling ways.

Moments drift, like clouds overhead,
In the gentle hush, let worries shed.
Dreams unfurl like blossoms in spring,
In a nest of moods, my heart can sing.

So linger here, in tender embrace,
In a nest of rest, find your place.
Let the night cradle you, steady and sweet,
In this sanctuary, let life retreat.

The Dawn's Cautious Return

The sun peeks o'er the hill,
A whisper on the breeze,
The world awakens still,
With gentle, golden tease.

The shadows fold and bend,
As colors start to rise,
A day begins again,
With painted, hopeful skies.

Birds sing their sweet refrain,
In chorus, soft and bright,
While dew drops on the grain,
Reflect the morning light.

This dance of light and dark,
A balance to behold,
The dawn leaves just a mark,
In hues of pink and gold.

Illusions of the Dreaming World

In twilight's gentle haze,
Where fantasies do dwell,
The mind begins to graze,
On stories it can tell.

A river made of stars,
Flows through the endless night,
With dreams of near and far,
That shimmer, soft and bright.

The whispers of the trees,
Invite us to explore,
Where time bends with the breeze,
And magic is in store.

Imagination flies,
On wings both strange and bold,
Within the mind's vast skies,
The dreams are manifold.

Cradled in Night's Embrace

The moon hangs low and bright,
In velvet's warm caress,
The world is wrapped in night,
In peaceful, quiet rest.

Stars twinkle like a smile,
On fabric deep and blue,
Each moment feels worthwhile,
As whispers drift anew.

The shadows softly play,
In corners yet unknown,
While time drifts far away,
In night, we're not alone.

With every breath, we find,
A solace in the dark,
Cradled by night, we're kind,
To dreams that leave a mark.

The Silent Dance of Shadows

In corners, shadows sway,
A secret, silent tune,
They merge, then drift away,
Beneath the watchful moon.

Each flicker tells a tale,
Of moments left behind,
As time begins to sail,
In whispers soft, confined.

With grace, they intertwine,
A ballet through the night,
Unseen, yet so divine,
In fluid, pure delight.

They vanish with the dawn,
The night's sweet symphony,
As light begins to spawn,
The dance fades silently.

Whispers of the Evening Star

In twilight's hush, the stars align,
A silver whisper, soft and fine.
The night unfolds its velvet cloak,
And dreams are born with every stroke.

The moon, a guardian in the dark,
Sends beams of light, a gentle spark.
While shadows dance on cool, still ground,
In silence, all our hopes are found.

The Palette of the Twilight Sky

Brushstrokes of pink and deepening blue,
Where the sun bids farewell to the view.
Golden hues blend with soft gray,
In twilight's embrace, night greets the day.

Clouds like shadows, drifting slow,
Carrying secrets the stars bestow.
Each color sings a gentle song,
In the twilight, we belong.

Repose of the Woven Dust

In corners dark, the dust lays still,
A tapestry of time, a quiet thrill.
Each particle tells a tale untold,
Of joys and sorrows, of warmth and cold.

A whisper echoes through the air,
Memories linger, heavy with care.
In repose, the world breathes deep,
In woven dust, our stories keep.

A Horizon of Gentle Dreaming

At dawn's first light, we find our way,
Through whispers of dreams that softly sway.
The horizon stretches, wide and bright,
Inviting hearts to take flight.

Clouds like brushstrokes dance above,
Painting paths of hope and love.
In gentle dreaming, we shall roam,
The horizon calls us softly home.

Fleeting Moments of Trance

In twilight's soft whisper, dreams unfold,
A dance of shadows, stories untold.
Time drips like honey, sweet and slow,
Caught in the moment, we let go.

The flickering flame casts a glow,
Memories linger, but tend to flow.
Lost in the rhythm of dreams that tease,
We breathe in the magic, find our ease.

Casting aside the weight of the day,
We glide on the waves, come what may.
In a trance so fleeting, we sway and spin,
Echoes of laughter, where love begins.

The Enchantment of Silent Hours

In the hush of the night, secrets take flight,
Stars become guardians, shining so bright.
Time holds its breath, wrapped in a shroud,
Whispers of dreams spin soft and loud.

The world fades away, a distant hum,
In silent hours, the heartbeats drum.
Thoughts intertwine like branches of trees,
In the stillness, we find our peace.

Moonlight slips gently, a silken embrace,
With each tender moment, we carve a space.
In the charm of the still, we learn to see,
The beauty of silence, the dance of the free.

Cradled by the Night's Breath

Wrapped in darkness, cradled so near,
Night's gentle breath, a whisper we hear.
Stars serenade, a lullaby sweet,
In the warm shadows, our hearts greet.

The moon casts her glow, a silver tide,
In the embrace of night, we softly bide.
Dreams bloom like flowers, bold and bright,
Cradled in comfort, wrapped in the night.

Time slows around us, we drift and roam,
Finding in silence, the heart finds home.
In the night's caress, worries subside,
Held by a promise that love can't hide.

Elysium Beneath the Stars

In the realm of night, magic lies,
Beneath the stars, a world that flies.
Glimmers of hope in the cosmic sea,
Whispers of wonder, just you and me.

Galaxies swirl, a dance so grand,
Infinite stories by fate's own hand.
With every heartbeat, we weave our thread,
In this elysium, where dreams are fed.

Hold tight to the moments that shimmer and gleam,
In the fabric of night, we find our dream.
Together we wander, through stardust and awe,
Under the vastness, we revere the law.

Feathered Veils of Repose

In the quiet of twilight's breath,
Whispers dance in gentle wane,
Feathered dreams on pillows rest,
Softly draped in night's domain.

Stars blink down, soft and bright,
As shadows weave their calm embrace,
While thoughts like drifting clouds take flight,
Suspended in this sacred space.

The world outside fades away,
Wrapped in warmth of midnight's sigh,
In this moment, let us stay,
As feathered veils blanket the sky.

Holding tight to dreams unfurled,
A tapestry of night and day,
In the stillness of our world,
Feathered veils guide us to play.

The Gentle Descent into Stillness

Beneath the glow of moonlit sheen,
A lullaby begins to play,
The world around, a tranquil scene,
Invites the heart to drift away.

With every sigh, the burdens melt,
As calmness wraps like a warm shawl,
In stillness, all our fears are dealt,
Eclipsed by night's serene enthrall.

As shadows blend and softly fade,
Embracing silence, we release,
In dreams' embrace, we're gently laid,
The descent brings the sweetest peace.

So close your eyes, let worries cease,
In this cocoon, let spirits soar,
The gentle descent grants us release,
We find our hearts forevermore.

Twilight's Caress

In the arms of twilight's glow,
Day and night embrace in dance,
A soothing breeze begins to flow,
As stars awaken, lost in trance.

Colors blend in soft array,
Painted skies, a canvas rare,
With whispers sweet, the night does sway,
In twilight's caress, dreams prepare.

Time slows down beneath the haze,
Where worries fade to fleeting mist,
We're captured in this golden blaze,
As fleeting moments can't be missed.

So let us bask in twilight's kiss,
With hearts aglow, we'll gently rest,
In nature's arms, we find our bliss,
As night enfolds us, truly blessed.

Sleep's Velvet Tapestry

In the shadows, dreams begin,
Woven deep in silence thick,
Every thought a gentle spin,
As sleep's design plays its trick.

Threads of night, a soothing blend,
Wrap us in their soft embrace,
With every sigh, the hours mend,
In this perfect, tranquil space.

Stars align like secret signs,
A map of wishes long untold,
Through velvet nights, each heart entwines,
In sleep's embrace, we feel consoled.

So let the world drift far away,
In this woven peace, we'll stay,
Bathed in dreams where spirits play,
Sleep's velvet tapestry at bay.

Scents of the Night Bloom

In the garden where shadows dance,
Fragrant whispers of night enhance.
Petals softly drink the dew,
Under the moon's tender view.

Lilies sway in a gentle breeze,
Carrying secrets through the trees.
Night-blooming jasmine's sweet perfume,
Wraps the world in a soft cocoon.

Stars shimmer with the softest light,
Guiding wanderers into the night.
Nature's chorus begins to sing,
In the arms of the night, we cling.

As the clock strikes midnight's tune,
Hearts are lifted, like the moon.
In this moment, we are free,
Lost in night's sweet harmony.

Swaying with the Nightingale

Beneath the oak, a melody flows,
A nightingale sings to the rose.
Each note twirls in the cool night air,
Swaying gently, without a care.

Stars wink softly in tune with thrush,
While fireflies dance in a golden hush.
Each whisper of wind tells a tale,
As shadows fade and dreams unveil.

The moon casts silver on the ground,
Night's embrace is a velvet shroud.
With every warble, hearts entwine,
As music drifts through space and time.

In this symphony of the night,
We find our souls taking flight.
Together, lost in the song's embrace,
Swaying gently, in timeless grace.

Enveloping in the Crescent Glow

A crescent moon in the velvet sky,
Whispers softly, as stars reply.
Golden beams on the river flow,
Enveloping all in a gentle glow.

Crickets serenade the cooling night,
Filling the air with pure delight.
The world, a canvas painted bright,
Under the spell of the soft moonlight.

While branches sway with whispered lore,
Night unfolds, revealing more.
Each shadow dances to the tune,
In harmony with the glowing moon.

For in this hour, magic's spun,
Two hearts awaken, as one.
Lost in dreams, the night unfurls,
In the embrace of silver pearls.

The Tinge of Dusk's Promise

A brush of colors paints the sky,
As day bids night a soft goodbye.
Golden hues intermingle and blend,
The tinge of dusk, where moments mend.

Whispers of warmth linger still,
Fading light, a tranquil thrill.
The horizon glows with a tender sigh,
As the sun dips low and time slips by.

In twilight's grasp, dreams take flight,
Beneath the stars that shine so bright.
Each heartbeat echoes the night's spell,
In dusk, we find our stories to tell.

With every shadow, hopes arise,
In the curtain of night, beneath the skies.
The promise of dawn, softly unfurls,
As dusk wraps the world in its pearls.

A Silent Voyage through the Stars

In the stillness of the night,
We drift beyond the glow,
Where whispers of the cosmos
Guide the path we know.

Stars like diamonds scattered wide,
Each a story, bright and bold,
We navigate the vast sea,
In dreams, our hearts unfold.

Galaxies in endless dance,
A waltz of light and grace,
The pulse of time surrounding,
In this celestial space.

With every breath, a journey,
In the silence, we are one,
A voyage through infinity,
Beneath the watchful sun.

Reveries in the Moon's Light

Underneath the silver glow,
Whispers of the night arise,
Dreams take flight on gentle winds,
Beneath the painted skies.

Softly sings the evening breeze,
Carrying secrets untold,
In the moonlight's tender embrace,
Eager hearts unfold.

Reflections dance upon the lake,
As shadows start to play,
Each moment holds a promise,
In the stillness of the day.

With every flicker, stories weave,
In the tapestry of night,
We find our place in starry realms,
As dreams take flight in light.

Embracing the Softness of Dark

In the quiet of the night,
Where shadows gently breathe,
We find solace in the dark,
And allow ourselves to leave.

Softly wrapped in velvet hues,
The world fades to a murmur,
In the arms of starry skies,
We find our hearts grow firmer.

Embracing all the unknowns,
As starlit thoughts collide,
The beauty of the darkness calls,
In it, we can confide.

With every sigh, the night responds,
A lullaby so sweet,
In the softness of the dark,
Our restless souls can meet.

Tides of a Nighttime Pulse

Moonlit waves caress the shore,
As whispers tug the mind,
The rhythm of the ocean breathes,
A heartbeat intertwined.

With every crash, a story told,
In echoes from afar,
The dance of tides, both wild and free,
Beneath the evening star.

In the quietude of night,
The pulse begins to swell,
As dreams take form and drift away,
In an ocean's gentle spell.

We ride the waves of shadowed time,
With thoughts like ships that sail,
In the nighttime's soft embrace,
Our hearts will never fail.

Whispers of Nightfall

The sun dips low, a soft goodbye,
Stars begin to wink, scattered in the sky.
Shadows lengthen, secrets softly creep,
In the hush of dark, the world goes deep.

Moonlight weaves through branches bare,
A silver thread in the cool night air.
Echoes of dreams float on the breeze,
Crickets sing softly among the trees.

Whispers of nightfall, gentle and true,
Wrapped in a cloak of midnight blue.
The heart finds peace in the twilight's embrace,
As the night unfolds its serene grace.

With every breath, the stillness sings,
In the quiet hours, the soul takes wing.
Night calls softly, a comforting muse,
In the twilight's whisper, the heart renews.

Feathered Embrace of Dusk

As the sun surrenders, colors ignite,
Birds take to flight in the fading light.
A canvas of hues, exquisite and vast,
Painting the sky as the day drifts past.

Dusk wraps the world in tender embrace,
A feathered touch in this tranquil space.
Whispers of wind carry dreams away,
To the arms of night, where shadows play.

Stars awaken, twinkling above,
In the quiet, there's a sense of love.
Nature's lullaby hums soft and low,
Guiding us gently where secrets flow.

Feathered embrace, a moment divine,
In the dusk's allure, our hearts intertwine.
A symphony woven with grace and light,
Carried on whispers of the night.

Lullabies of the Twilight Sky

In the twilight sky, the colors blend,
Crimson and gold as the daylight ends.
Clouds like whispers, drift soft and slow,
Each moment lingers, a sweet glow.

Lullabies echo from a fading sun,
As day and night meld, two worlds become one.
The horizon hums a soothing tune,
Beneath the watchful eye of the moon.

Stars twinkle softly, like little eyes,
Watching the hush of the night arise.
The world exhales, in a calming sigh,
Embraced by the magic of the twilight sky.

In every corner, quiet dreams unfold,
Stories of wonder, waiting to be told.
Beneath the blanket of the deepening night,
Lullabies soar in the soft starlight.

Dreams on Gentle Breezes

On gentle breezes, dreams take flight,
Whispers of wishes in the deepening night.
Clouds drift lazily, soft as cotton,
Bringing forth visions, both sweet and forgotten.

Echoes of laughter, a soothing song,
In the quiet of dusk, where hearts belong.
Stars sprinkle hope like grains of sand,
Lighting the way to a promised land.

With every sigh, the night unfolds,
Stories of magic and wonders untold.
The world slows down, a tender pause,
In dreams wrapped softly, beneath the stars.

So let your heart dance on breezes light,
Where dreams awaken and take their flight.
In this serene canvas, let your soul rest,
For on gentle breezes, we are truly blessed.

Where Dreams Take Flight

In twilight's glow, the stars ignite,
Whispers of hope take gentle flight.
Beneath the moon's enchanting caress,
In dreams we wander, we find our rest.

Off in the distance, a soft wind sighs,
Carrying wishes, where magic lies.
Through fields of silver, our spirits roam,
In the heart of night, we find our home.

With every heartbeat, a new path unfolds,
Stories of courage and love retold.
Each fleeting moment, a gift on our way,
Where dreams take flight at the end of the day.

As dawn approaches, the shadows cease,
A tapestry woven, we find our peace.
And though it fades, we hold it tight,
In the sacred stillness of the night.

A Slumbering Serenade

Softly the night wraps its arms around,
In silence and stillness, serene sound.
The lullabies of twilight begin,
Cradling the weary, inviting them in.

Moonlight drapes the world in silver lace,
Dreams gently beckon, a hallowed space.
With every breath, the night expands,
In the cradle of stars, we soar, we land.

Close your eyes tight, let worries fade,
A symphony plays in the cool night shade.
Harmonies woven from whispers of old,
A slumbering serenade, sweet and bold.

From dusk till dawn, let visions unfold,
A tapestry rich with stories untold.
As dawn's light breaks, the dreams take flight,
In the heart of the night, everything feels right.

Night's Embrace enfolds

In twilight's arms, we find our peace,
A world asleep, as moments cease.
Shadows dance beneath the stars,
In night's embrace, we heal our scars.

The stillness whispers ancient tales,
Of distant lands and whispered gales.
Through silent woods, the echoes roam,
Where weary hearts can finally come home.

With every breath, the night unfolds,
Together weaving dreams like gold.
In the hush of midnight's quiet grace,
Night's embrace enfolds, a warm embrace.

As darkness deepens, we lose our fears,
Cradled softly in hopes and years.
Tender and sweet, this magic allows,
To rest our souls and renew our vows.

The Restful Reverie

In depths of night, where shadows play,
We drift on clouds, let worries sway.
A gentle breeze through open blinds,
The restful reverie of peaceful minds.

Stars twinkle softly, a cosmic dance,
Inviting the dreamers to take a chance.
With each heartbeat, we flow and glide,
Through realms of wonder, side by side.

Close your tired eyes, drift away,
Let the dreams call, let the heart sway.
In a tapestry woven from whispers and sighs,
The restful reverie never dies.

As dawn approaches, let soft light break,
A promise renewed with each day we make.
In the silence of night, we weave and bind,
In the restful reverie, solace we find.

Swirling in Gentle Haze

In twilight's blush, the shadows dance,
Whispers weave in a soft expanse.
The world blurs in golden light,
As day surrenders to the night.

Breezes carry sweet perfume,
Muffling all the loud and gloom.
Colors fade into a sigh,
As dreams take flight, and spirits fly.

In circles spun with grace and ease,
Time slows down, my mind's appease.
The calmness washes over me,
A gentle tide, a soothing spree.

With every breath, I feel the sway,
In gentle hues, I drift away.
A swirl of thoughts, both light and free,
In this soft haze, I find my glee.

Echoes of a Distant Dream

In morning's glow, a hint of light,
Whispers call from past's delight.
A melody of lost embrace,
A fleeting thought in time's vast space.

Through shadows deep, my heart does roam,
In distant realms, I find my home.
A soft reminder of what has been,
In echoes sweet, the silence kin.

With every step on dew-kissed grass,
The memories swirl, they come to pass.
Fragments of laughter fill the air,
In woven threads of love and care.

As twilight falls and stars ignite,
I chase the dreams that haunt the night.
In gentle whispers, they unfold,
The stories waiting to be told.

Floating on Clouded Thoughts

Upon the breeze, a sigh drifts slow,
Emotions rise, as soft winds blow.
Thoughts like clouds in soft array,
They linger there, then drift away.

In wisps of white, my mind does play,
Creating worlds where I may stay.
Floating high, so light and free,
Where wishes are and dreams can be.

A canvas vast, with hues unbound,
In this soft realm, lost dreams are found.
Each gentle thought a feathered kiss,
In clouded realms, I find my bliss.

With every breath of air so sweet,
I dance on clouds, where heartbeats meet.
And as I rise in skies above,
I float on thoughts, I dream of love.

Resting on Velvet Clouds

As day gives way to starry night,
I find a peace, a soft respite.
On velvet clouds, my body lays,
In soft embrace of twilight's glaze.

The world below fades far away,
In stillness found, I softly stay.
With whispered dreams, the night unfolds,
In warmth of dusk, my heart beholds.

Stars flicker like the dreams inside,
As I let go, the fears subside.
A tranquil heart, a quiet mind,
In velvet clouds, my peace I find.

In cosmic arms, I drift and bend,
A gentle journey without end.
Resting here, so soft and free,
On velvet clouds, I long to be.

Cozy Cocoon of Night

Wrapped in shadows, whispers low,
Stars above in soft aglow.
Moonbeams dance on silken sheets,
In this nest, my heart retreats.

Crickets sing a lullaby's tune,
Embracing dreams, we drift like the moon.
Time slows down, no need for haste,
In this cocoon, pure love encased.

Twinkling lights in the velvet sky,
Every worry scattered, gone awry.
Nestled deep, my soul takes flight,
In the cozy cocoon of night.

Silence wraps like a gentle shawl,
Binding dreams where shadows fall.
Heartbeats whisper, soft and bright,
In this warmth, we find our light.

Tender Embrace of Nightfall

As twilight wraps the world in grace,
Stars emerge, a soft embrace.
Whispers float on gentle air,
In this moment, hearts laid bare.

The horizon blushes, lights descend,
Moonlit paths where dreams extend.
Crickets pause, the world takes breath,
In tender night, we talk of death.

Holding hands beneath the skies,
Gazing deep into your eyes.
Nightfall brings a quiet peace,
In this love, sweet moments cease.

Wrapped in silence, still we rest,
Chest to chest, I feel your best.
Shadows dance, the stars alight,
In your arms, the world feels right.

Driftwood of Dreams

A forgotten shore, the tides entwine,
Driftwood whispers stories of time.
Each grain a memory, soft and light,
Waves of dreams fade into night.

Carried on currents, hopes afloat,
Lost in the sea, a fragile boat.
The salty air, a gentle tease,
Washing over, like a breeze.

Flickering flames by the ocean's edge,
Echoing tales of eternity's pledge.
Stars reflect on water's skin,
In this moment, new dreams begin.

With every wave, the past renews,
Driftwood of dreams in golden hues.
Embrace the night, let spirits soar,
Find the shore where souls explore.

The Quiet Serenade of Rest

In the stillness, night descends,
A quiet serenade, nature lends.
Crickets play a gentle song,
In this peace, we all belong.

Pillows soft where dreams reside,
With twilight's hush, we gently glide.
Wrapped in warmth, the world at bay,
In slumber's arms, we drift away.

The stars twinkle, a fleeting sigh,
Evening whispers, a lullaby.
Heartbeats sync with night's embrace,
In the dark, we find our space.

Rest your head, let worries cease,
In the quiet, find your peace.
Tomorrow waits with open arms,
But for now, night holds its charms.

Echoes of a Dreamscape

In the hush of twilight's stretch,
Whispers of wishes softly beck,
Moonlit shadows dance in grace,
Echoes linger, a gentle trace.

Colors swirl in a dreamer's mind,
Lost in realms we cannot find,
Stars above, a guiding light,
Guiding hearts through endless night.

Softly drifting, time stands still,
In a world where dreams fulfill,
Every heartbeat sings a song,
In this place where we belong.

Awake or sleeping, all's the same,
In this dance, we lose the name,
Only echoes, shadows play,
In the dreamscape, we shall stay.

Cloudy Pillows at Dusk

Pillows rise like clouds above,
Cushions of dreams wrapped in love,
As the sun begins to fade,
Whispers weave in twilight's shade.

Gentle breezes softly sigh,
As colors melt into the sky,
Mellow hues, a painter's hand,
Crafting worlds where we can stand.

Each heartbeat drifts on softest air,
Cloudy pillows, free from care,
Floating dreams in twilight's glow,
Every secret that we know.

Time dissolves in evening's grace,
Wrapped in warmth, we find our place,
In the shadows, silence plays,
Cloudy pillows, endless days.

Moonbeam Melodies

Beneath the stars, soft tunes arise,
Moonbeam whispers cross the skies,
Every note a silver thread,
Woven tales of dreams widespread.

Gentle glimmers paint the night,
Melodies of pure delight,
In the quiet, hearts ignite,
Dancing softly, taking flight.

Where the shadows softly sway,
Underneath the moon's soft ray,
Every sound, a sweet caress,
In this world, we find our rest.

Catch the echoes of the night,
As the stars begin their flight,
Moonbeam songs will guide our way,
Through the twilight, come what may.

Slumber's Embrace

In the cradle of the night,
Slumber wraps us, pure and light,
Close your eyes, release the day,
In this realm, we drift away.

Softly rocking, dreams take flight,
In the shadows, hearts unite,
Every heartbeat, calm and slow,
In this space, love's gentle glow.

Whispers of a distant shore,
Echo softly evermore,
Through the silence, peace we find,
In slumber's arms, we intertwine.

As the world begins to rest,
Wrapped in warmth, we are blessed,
In the night, our dreams embrace,
With the stars, we find our place.

Glimmering Veils of Calm

Beneath the twilight's gentle glow,
A peace that softly starts to grow.
Whispers dance on zephyr's breath,
Each moment holds a whispered death.

Stars shimmer in the velvet night,
Casting dreams in silver light.
The world, a canvas, tranquil and bright,
Wraps the heart in pure delight.

In shadows deep, the silence dwells,
Where no one speaks, yet all compels.
The moon, a guardian, watches over,
Guiding souls like a serene rover.

Time drifts on in slow embrace,
Each heartbeat finds its rightful place.
In glimmering veils, we find our way,
To calm the storms of the day.

The Chime of Midnight Whispers

As midnight strikes, the chimes awake,
Soft echoes through the night partake.
Whispers weave in shadows cast,
In secrets shared, the die is cast.

The moonlight spills on dreams untold,
In every flicker, stories fold.
An eternal dance, the stars align,
With every breath, the worlds entwine.

Thoughts like feathers drift and sway,
Into the night, they find their way.
With every chime, a promise made,
Where silence lingers, fears will fade.

In this hour, when stillness reigns,
The heart can shed its heavy chains.
As shadows whisper softly near,
In midnight's arms, we lose our fear.

A Glimpse into the Dreamworld

A canvas spun of silver light,
Where thoughts take flight in pure delight.
From earthly ties, our spirits soar,
Beyond the waves, to distant shores.

In dreamworld's arms, all colors blend,
With whispered hopes that never end.
Each moment, a fleeting embrace,
A place where time holds no trace.

Guardians of dreams, silent and wise,
Guide us through starlit skies.
In this realm, all fears dissolve,
In unity, we long evolve.

A glimpse revealed, a life unbound,
In this world, peace is found.
As dawn approaches, dreams may fade,
Yet in our hearts, their magic stayed.

Veils of Serenity

In every breath, a gentle pause,
A time to cherish, just because.
Through veils of serenity, we find,
A quiet space for heart and mind.

Golden rays of sunlight spill,
Over valleys, soft and still.
Nature's song, a soothing balm,
In every note, we find our calm.

Gentle waves caress the shore,
Whispering tales of ancient lore.
Each ripple speaks of love's embrace,
A moment's gift, a sacred space.

As twilight drapes the earth in grace,
We travel to a tranquil place.
Bathed in love, we rise above,
In veils of serenity, we dwell in love.

Restful Reveries

In the quiet of the night,
Dreams begin to take flight.
Gentle thoughts softly flow,
Where the weary hearts go.

Stars sprinkle the sky wide,
Whispers of peace collide.
In shadows, secrets unfold,
Stories waiting to be told.

A gentle breeze sings low,
Carrying tales from below.
The moon bathes all in light,
Wrapping us warm tonight.

As time drifts slowly by,
We close our weary eyes.
In restful reveries, we find,
A solace of the mind.

Ethereal Drift of the Mind

Thoughts like clouds float high,
In a vast and endless sky.
Colors merge and blur anew,
In an ethereal hue.

Minds drift on a gentle stream,
In the cradle of a dream.
Fleeting moments intertwine,
Woven in the fabric fine.

Each sigh carries a wish,
Wrapped in a soft, sweet bliss.
Mysteries of the heart sway,
In the dawn of a new day.

So let your spirit roam free,
Let it dance, let it be.
In this tranquil, sacred space,
Find your heart's resting place.

Surrendering to the Night

As twilight descends with grace,
All the worries find their place.
Embracing shadows, we sway,
Surrendering to the night's play.

Stars emerge with a gentle glow,
Whispering secrets only they know.
In this quiet, we lay down,
Letting go of the day's crown.

Hushed are the sounds of the street,
In the dark, the heart feels sweet.
Wrapped in a blanket of peace,
Letting every tension cease.

So breathe in the night's cool air,
Feel the magic everywhere.
In surrender, we find delight,
In the embrace of the night.

Night's Gentle Whisper

A soft voice calls from afar,
Echoing under the star.
Night's gentle whisper draws near,
Filling the soul with cheer.

Crickets sing a lullaby,
While the moon watches high.
Every rustle, every sound,
In this stillness, we are bound.

Sleep's tender arms embrace,
In this calm and sacred space.
The world fades, worries cease,
In the night, we find our peace.

So let us listen close,
To the night's sweet, soft prose.
In its whispers, we will find,
The solace of the mind.

A Voyage into Quietude

In the hush of dawn, we sail,
Soft whispers guide the gentle trail.
Stars retreat, the sun will rise,
Calmness woven in the skies.

Waves lap gently at the shore,
Old dreams stir; they call for more.
Embrace the stillness, let it flow,
In quietude, our spirits grow.

With each breath, the world seems clear,
Echoes fade, no need for fear.
Drifting softly through the day,
In tranquil waters, we will stay.

A voyage made in search of peace,
In silence, all our worries cease.
Come sail with me, and you will find,
A treasure trove of a peaceful mind.

Nighttime's Secret Garden

In shadows where the moonlight glows,
A hidden realm of dreams bestows.
Flowers bloom with silver hues,
Their fragrance dances in the blues.

Whispers of the night unfold,
Secrets in the air, untold.
Crickets sing their softest song,
Inviting all to linger long.

Stars above like lanterns bright,
Guide the wanderer through the night.
Each step leads to wonders rare,
In nighttime's garden, magic's there.

The breeze, a gentle lover's sigh,
Wraps the soul as dreams drift by.
In this haven, let us roam,
Nighttime's garden feels like home.

The Ethereal Drift

On clouds adorned with twilight's lace,
We glide through realms of time and space.
Floating softly, hearts align,
In the drift, the stars are mine.

As whispers of the cosmos play,
We drift and dance, night turns to day.
With every pulse, the universe sighs,
In this embrace, our spirits rise.

The moon's gaze warms our destined path,
A journey free from stormy wrath.
In cosmic winds, our thoughts can soar,
The ethereal drift opens doors.

All burdens shed, we find our flight,
In endless skies, the heart feels right.
Together lost, yet never missed,
In the drift, we truly exist.

Celestial Repose

Beneath the arch of endless night,
Stars gather round, a wondrous sight.
In cosmic arms, we find our grace,
In celestial repose, we embrace.

The heavens whisper secrets low,
An astral lullaby to bestow.
Gentle breezes weave a tune,
Underneath the watchful moon.

Time stands still in this sacred space,
Galaxies spin at a gentle pace.
Hearts align with the universe wide,
In this repose, love cannot hide.

So let us rest, in dreams we trust,
In celestial light, our souls adjust.
Together bound in stardust ways,
In this peaceful glow, our hearts will blaze.

Serene Shadows of Slumber

In the quiet night so deep,
Whispers drift where dreamers sleep.
Softly wrapped in twilight's grace,
Time stands still in this embrace.

Silent tales the shadows weave,
In their arms, we dare believe.
Every sigh lost to the air,
Holding magic everywhere.

Gentle breezes brush the ground,
In this peace, no fears are found.
Stars above begin to wane,
In the light, dreams dance like rain.

Sleepy eyes begin to close,
Cradled by the night that glows.
Serene shadows, calm and bright,
Guide us through the velvet night.

Silken Caress of Rest

Feathered whispers touch the skin,
As twilight settles deep within.
Each heartbeat slows its racing song,
In the hush, we all belong.

Dreams unfold like petals wide,
Bathed in warmth, we safely bide.
Silken sheets and pillows soft,
Lift us high, in clouds aloft.

Moonbeams dance on slumbered breath,
Painting peace, defying death.
Gentle strokes of night's caress,
In this calm, we find our rest.

Close your eyes to all the day,
Let the stars simply sway.
In this moment, we are free,
Wrapped in tranquility.

Murmurs of the Moonlit Hour

Silver beams whisper on the lake,
Rippling softly, no need to wake.
In the stillness, secrets flow,
As the night begins to glow.

Murmurs drift on gentle air,
Carried forth without a care.
Each soft sound, a lullaby,
Filling dreams that drift on high.

Shadows dance upon the ground,
Echoes of the silence found.
Every glance at starlit skies,
Spins a world where magic lies.

Time suspends in silver light,
Capturing the heart of night.
Murmurs soft as lovers' sighs,
Lead us where our spirit flies.

Hush of the Starlit Veil

Underneath the starlit sky,
Whispers linger, soft and shy.
Hush now, let the quiet speak,
Finding solace in the meek.

The world fades in night's embrace,
Hearts find peace in hidden space.
Every star a glimmered dream,
Woven tight in moonlight's beam.

Cloaked in darkness, fears will fade,
In this hush, we are remade.
Silken shadows gently fall,
A tender balm to soothe us all.

Wrap us in the night's deep hold,
Softly wrapped in stories told.
Hush of night, divine and wild,
Lulls the heart, the spirit, child.

A Symphony of Asleep

In twilight's gentle embrace, the world sighs,
Moonlight dances softly on closed eyes.
Whispers of dreams weave through the night,
As silence cradles the stars' quiet light.

A lullaby hums in the cool evening air,
With every heartbeat, a calm thread we share.
Time drifts softly on wings of sweet peace,
In slumber's warm grasp, all worries cease.

Through shadows that glide like a soft feather,
We find solace in thoughts that tether.
Each moment a note in the symphony's scheme,
A tapestry woven of hope and of dream.

Hushed Secrets of the Dark

In the quiet fold of night's tender blush,
Secrets linger in shadows: a hush.
The moon holds court over hidden desires,
While stars keep watch, igniting their fires.

Echoes of whispers weave tales so old,
In the stillness, mysteries gently unfold.
The dark cradles stories, both ancient and new,
As hearts beat softly, concealed from view.

Each breath is a vow, a promise unspoken,
In the silence, the bonds are never broken.
Embrace what's concealed in the quiet of night,
For within the dark lies a glimmer of light.

The Tapestry of Dusk

The sun dips low, stitching day into night,
A tapestry glows with colors so bright.
Threads of orange, pink, and gold,
Weave stories of silence, both brave and bold.

Breezes carry whispers of twilight's embrace,
As shadows collect, filling open space.
Each leaf rustles softly, a note in the song,
Nature's own chorus, where all things belong.

With every stroke of the fading light,
The fabric of dusk bids the day goodnight.
Hope lingers softly in amber-hued skies,
As the stars unveil their welcoming eyes.

Driftwood Dreams

Upon the shore where the wild waves play,
Driftwood gathers stories from each passing day.
Weathered and worn, each piece tells a tale,
Of journeys untold and storms that prevail.

Carried by currents, they wander so free,
In sepia visions, a life yet to see.
The ocean's embrace sings songs of the past,
As memories linger, forever to last.

Underneath starlight, they nestle and rest,
In dreams woven softly, a timeless quest.
From land to sea, where they drift and they glide,
The heart of the ocean stands open wide.

Lull of the Echoing Woods

Whispers drift through ancient trees,
Softly sung by evening's breeze.
Moonlight dapples on the ground,
Nature's calmness all around.

Crickets chirp a soothing tune,
Beneath the watchful silver moon.
Leaves dance lightly, shadows play,
In the heart of night's ballet.

Branches sway in gentle grace,
Every creature finds its place.
Silence holds a sacred space,
As dreams begin to interlace.

In the woods where echoes blend,
Even twilight seems to mend.
Close your eyes, let worries fade,
In this tranquil, woodland glade.

The Gossamer Thread of Nightfall

When daylight bows to evening's call,
A gossamer thread begins to sprawl.
Stars awaken, a twinkling show,
As the softest shadows grow.

A velvet cloak wraps the land tight,
Guiding dreams into the night.
With every whisper, moments blend,
Time and space seem to suspend.

Beneath the cloak, secrets twine,
Wonder lingers, soft and fine.
Nightfall weaves a magic rare,
In the silence, hearts lay bare.

Threads of silver, spun with grace,
Embrace the quiet, seek your place.
In the dark, let spirits rise,
Finding peace beneath the skies.

Reflections in Still Water

In tranquil pools, the world is caught,
A mirrored dance of dreams we sought.
Ripples form with gentle sighs,
Each one telling silent lies.

Beneath the surface, secrets lie,
Where whispers float and shadows fly.
Mountains stand with dignity,
Captured in this harmony.

The sky blushes with hues of gold,
As stories of the day unfold.
Clouds drift softly, a transient dream,
In still water, life's current streams.

Heart and moment intertwine,
In reflections, truths align.
Pause awhile, let your heart see,
The grace of what it means to be.

Mysterious Paths to Twilight

Winding trails through elder trees,
Lead us where the heart finds ease.
Shadows merge with fading light,
On the brink of coming night.

Footsteps echo soft and low,
As the twilight starts to glow.
Every turn, a tale unfolds,
Of whispered dreams and secrets told.

Faintly glimmers, the path ahead,
Guided by the stars widespread.
In this dusk, a magic stirs,
Through the forest, wonder whirs.

Take a breath, let worries cease,
Feel the warmth of nature's peace.
Mysterious paths, we roam with grace,
In twilight's arms, we find our place.

A Pillow of Stars

In the velvet sky we lay,
Counting dreams that drift away.
Each star a word, a whispered prayer,
A tapestry of wishes rare.

The moonlight dances on our skin,
A gentle touch where love begins.
Each twinkle holds a secret bright,
A comfort found in the night.

Cradled by the cosmic hush,
In the stillness, hearts do rush.
We find our peace, our place to rest,
A haven in the universe's chest.

With every sigh, we share our fate,
In this embrace, we contemplate.
A pillow made of stardust dreams,
In the darkness, hope always gleams.

The Silence Between Heartbeats

In the quiet, we find our way,
Where words falter, silence stays.
A moment held, a breath so sweet,
In this stillness, our hearts meet.

Time suspends, a fragile thread,
In the space where thoughts are bred.
An echo soft, a sacred pause,
In silence, love finds its cause.

Every heartbeat tells a tale,
In whispers soft, where dreams prevail.
A gentle pact, unspoken bond,
In the silence, we respond.

So let the moments linger long,
In stillness, we are ever strong.
For in between each thumping sound,
Is where our truest selves are found.

Surrendering to the Night

As dusk unfurls its velvet cloak,
A gentle hush, the stars provoke.
We lay our burdens at the door,
And step into the night once more.

With each breath, we let it go,
The day's bright chaos turns to flow.
In shadows deep, our spirits soar,
In surrender, we crave more.

The moon casts light on whispered fears,
In the dark, we shed our tears.
Each secret shared, a soft embrace,
In the night, we find our place.

So let the darkness wrap us tight,
In surrender, we take flight.
For in the stillness of this hour,
We blossom like a midnight flower.

Feathered Thoughts in the Ether

Like whispers carried on the breeze,
Thoughts take flight, they twist and tease.
Each feathered dream that flits away,
Glimmers like gold at break of day.

In the ether, ideas bloom,
Softly dancing, dispelling gloom.
With every thought, a story spins,
A journey starts, a soul begins.

They wander worlds, both far and near,
In every moment, crystal clear.
Each feather light, a passage free,
In the mind, where hearts can see.

So let them soar, these thoughts of grace,
In the quiet, find your place.
For in the ether, dreams take wing,
And in their flight, our spirits sing.

Milton Keynes UK
Ingram Content Group UK Ltd.
UKHW020735301124
451807UK00019B/791

The Veil of Sleep

In twilight's cloak, the world stands still,
A gentle hush, a soft goodwill.
The veil of sleep descends so light,
Whispers of dreams take flight tonight.

Stars twinkle softly, a lullaby sweet,
Cradled by night, where shadows meet.
In slumber's arms, we drift away,
Into realms where the heart can play.

Each dream a tapestry, woven tight,
Threads of gold in the tapestry of night.
Resting in peace, as worries cease,
Under the moon's watchful, loving peace.

As dawn embraces the sleeping land,
The veil of sleep slips from our hand.
Awake with grace, from night we leap,
Emerging anew from the veil of sleep.

Milton Keynes UK
Ingram Content Group UK Ltd.
UKHW030750121124
451094UK00013B/800

9 789916 889794